Oxford Elementary School

BLAZERS

SUPER SPEED

TRUCK
Racing

BY TRACY NELSON MAURER

Reading Consultant:
Barbara J. Fox
Reading Specialist
Professor Emerita
North Carolina State University

Content Consultant:
Rick Sosebee
Off-road Powersports Journalist
Dawsonville, Georgia

CAPSTONE PRESS
a capstone imprint

Blazers Books are published by Capstone Press,
1710 Roe Crest Drive, North Mankato, Minnesota 56003
www.capstonepub.com

Library of Congress Cataloging-in-Publication Data
Cataloging-in-publication information is on file with the Library of Congress.
ISBN 978-1-4765-0118-5 (library binding)
ISBN 978-1-4765-3366-7 (eBook PDF)

Editorial Credits
Kathryn Clay and Christopher L. Harbo, editors; Gene Bentdahl, designer;
Jennifer Walker, production specialist

Photo Credits
Alamy: Michael Doolittle, 22; AP Images: Autostock/Russell LaBounty, cover; Big Rig Drag Racing
– St-Joseph de Beauce, 27; Newscom: Icon SMI/David Allio, 12-13, Icon SMI/David J. Griffin,
6-7, 29, Icon SMI/Marc Sanchez, 5, 16-17, Icon SMI/Worth Canoy, 11; Shutterstock: Action Sports
Photography, 14-15, 19, Barry Salmons, 20-21, Doug James, 8, EvrenKalinbacak, 25 (both)

Artistic Effects
Shutterstock: 1xpert, My Portfolio, rodho

The author extends truckloads of appreciation to Patrick Breitbach.

Oxford Elementary School

Printed in the United States of America in Stevens Point, Wisconsin.
032013   007227WZF13

TABLE OF CONTENTS

ROARING MACHINES

If race cars purr, then racing trucks roar. Their giant engines shake the ground as drivers wait for the starting flag. From pickups to semitrucks, these vehicles deliver blazing speed and raw power.

semitruck—a large truck typically used to pull a trailer

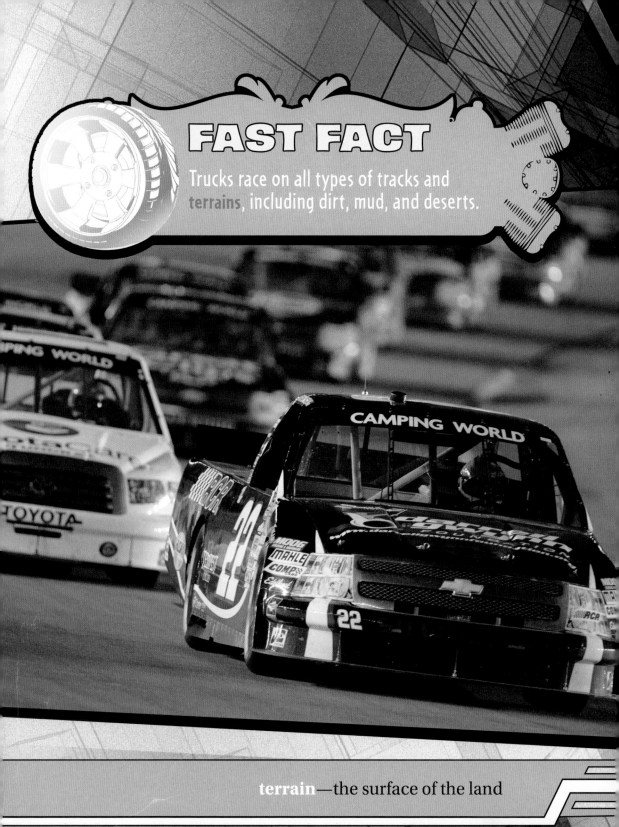

terrain—the surface of the land

FAST AND FIERCE NASCAR TRUCKS

The National Association for Stock Car Auto Racing (NASCAR) allows four mid-size trucks in its racing series. They are the Chevrolet Silverado, Toyota Tundra, Chrysler Ram, and Ford F-150.

FAST FACT

NASCAR truck racing began in 1995. More than one million fans attend truck races each year.

FAST FACT

NASCAR racing trucks weigh
3,400 pounds (1,540 kilograms).
They are about 1,100 pounds (500 kg)
lighter than street versions.

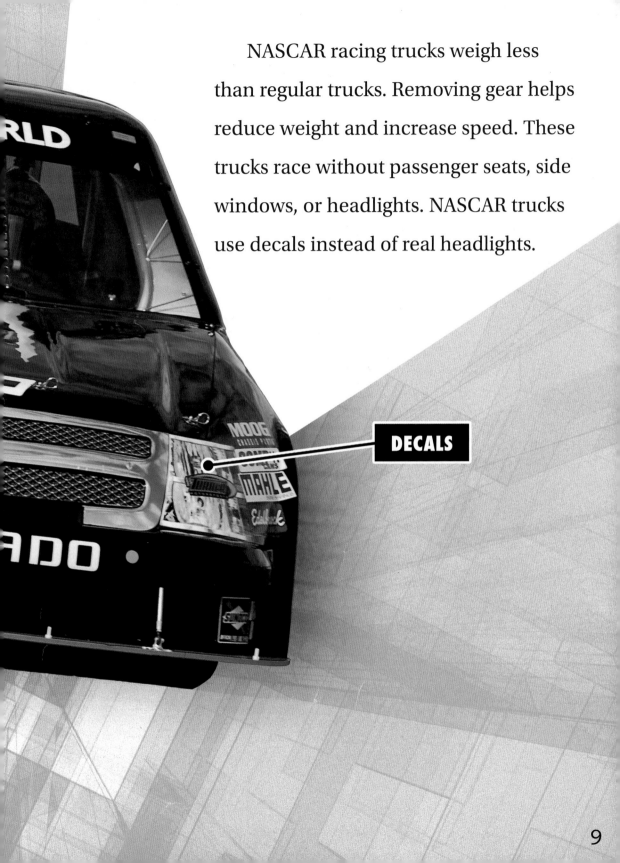

NASCAR racing trucks weigh less than regular trucks. Removing gear helps reduce weight and increase speed. These trucks race without passenger seats, side windows, or headlights. NASCAR trucks use decals instead of real headlights.

DECALS

NASCAR racing trucks ride low to the ground. Small 15-inch (38-centimeter) tires, called slicks, allow drivers to gain speed and maintain control.

FAST FACT

Some NASCAR racing trucks have hit speeds of 180 miles (290 km) per hour.

slick—a racing tire made with a smooth, soft surface to get a strong grip on the track

PHOTO DIAGRAM

1. AIR DAM
2. FRONT SPLITTER
3. SLICKS
4. SHATTER-PROOF WINDSHIELD
5. WINDOW NET
6. FUEL CELL
7. REAR SPOILER
8. BED COVER
9. CAB
10. ROLL CAGE

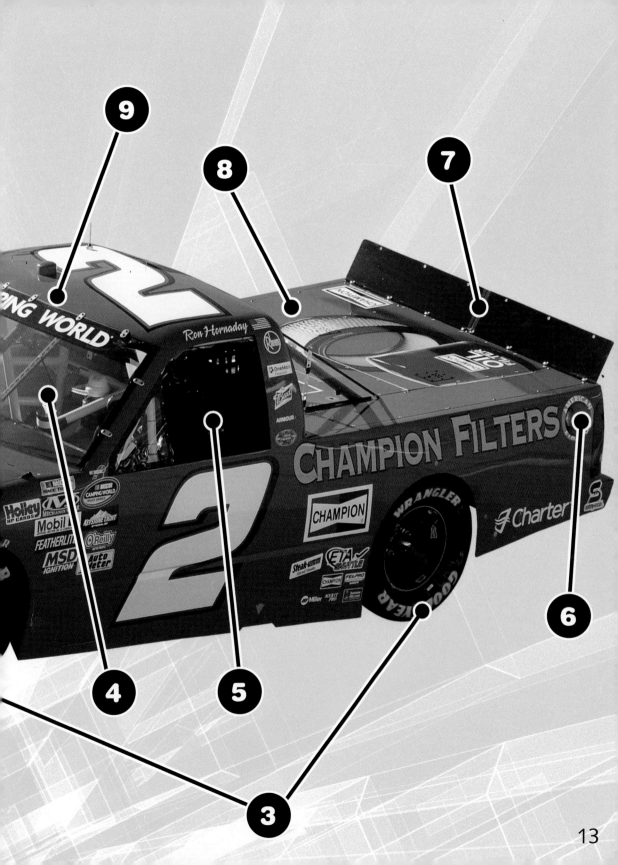

The NASCAR truck series features
22 races between February and
November at paved tracks across
the United States. Drivers complete
at least 100 laps at most tracks.

paved—when a road is covered with a hard
material such as concrete or asphalt

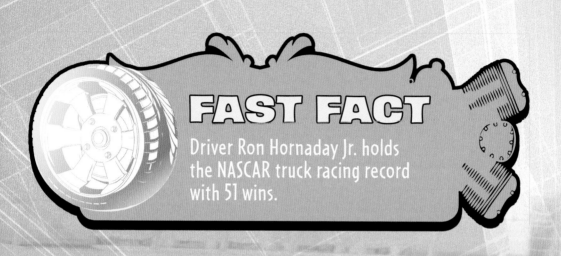

FAST FACT

Driver Ron Hornaday Jr. holds the NASCAR truck racing record with 51 wins.

Only 36 drivers qualify for each NASCAR race. Drivers earn points based on their finishing position. They earn bonus points for leading laps and for first-place finishes. The racer with the most points at the end of the season is the champion.

qualify—to earn a starting spot in a race; NASCAR truck drivers qualify by completing timed laps

LARGE AND LOUD

For some race fans, big trucks are best. Giant monster trucks launch off ramps and fly more than 35 feet (11 meters) through the air.

FAST FACT

Bob Chandler built the first monster truck in 1975. He named this truck Bigfoot. Chandler's Bigfoot trucks continue to be crowd favorites at monster truck shows.

Monster trucks race two at a time on short dirt tracks. They dodge or climb ramps, cars, and other objects that stand in their way.

FAST FACT

Most monster trucks travel about 20 to 30 miles (32 to 48 km) per hour. The world record monster truck speed is 93 miles (150 km) per hour.

Monster trucks stand about 12 feet (3.7 m) tall and weigh about 10,000 pounds (4,500 kg). Drivers must be careful when steering these giant machines. All drivers wear helmets, neck collars, and other safety gear.

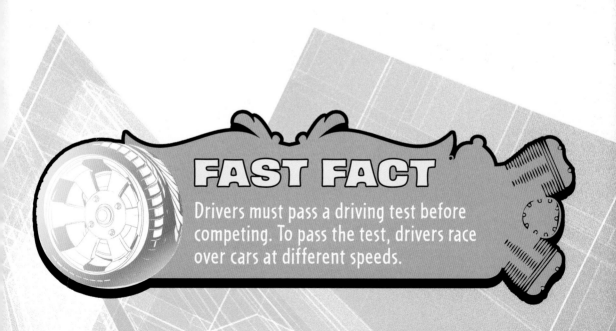

FAST FACT

Drivers must pass a driving test before competing. To pass the test, drivers race over cars at different speeds.

Super truck racing is another form of extreme racing. Huge semitrucks race on paved oval or winding tracks. Fans flock to see these 10,000-pound (4,500-kg) big rigs fly down the track.

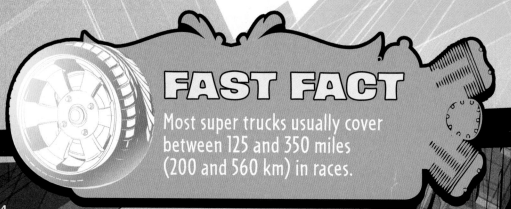

FAST FACT

Most super trucks usually cover between 125 and 350 miles (200 and 560 km) in races.

Some semitrucks compete in shorter drag races. A special gas mixture helps these giant trucks race down the drag strip. They reach speeds of 120 miles (193 km) per hour.

drag strip—a paved, straight track usually no more than 0.25 mile (0.4 km) long

CHARGING AHEAD

Truck racing is charging ahead with new designs for safety, speed, and power. Whether it's a small pickup or a huge semitruck, trucks have found a place in the racing spotlight.

FAST FACT

NASCAR's truck series is the third most-watched racing series on cable TV. It comes in just behind NASCAR's two national stock car series.

GLOSSARY

drag strip (DRAG STRIP)—a paved, straight track usually no more than 0.25 mile (0.4 km) long

paved (PAYVD)—when a road is covered with a hard material such as concrete or asphalt

qualify (KWAHL-uh-fye)—to earn a starting spot in a race; NASCAR truck drivers qualify by completing timed laps

semitruck (SEM-eye-truhk)—a large truck typically used to pull a trailer

slick (SLIK)—a racing tire made with a smooth, soft surface to get a strong grip on the track

terrain (tuh-RAYN)—the surface of the land

READ MORE

Polydoros, Lori. *Drag Racing.* Super Speed. North Mankato, Minn.: Capstone Press, 2013.

Sandler, Michael. *Dynamic Drag Racers.* Fast Rides. New York: Bearport Pub., 2011.

Savery, Annabel. *Supercars.* It's Amazing! Mankato, Minn.: Smart Apple Media, 2013.

INTERNET SITES

FactHound offers a safe, fun way to find Internet sites related to this book. All of the sites on FactHound have been researched by our staff.

Here's all you do:

Visit *www.facthound.com*

Type in this code: 9781476501185

Check out projects, games and lots more at
www.capstonekids.com

INDEX

Oxford Elementary School